MW01136891

WORKBOOK

The Complete Guide to Memory

By Richard Restak, MD

PithBooks

From: _____

To: _____

INTRODUCTION

Memory is everything. It is identity. Also, our identity is defined by our experiences. Memory is vital to brain enhancement and prevention of Alzheimer's disease and other dementias. These are reasons why we need to take care of our memory.

This workbook explains the evolution of memory, highlights the types of memory, and recommends ways of improving memory.

Through the pages that follow, you will put your memory to action and eventually improve its function.

ONE
WHY SHOULD I CARE ABOUT MY MEMORY?

Background

You should care about your memory. Why? Several reasons. One is that the memory is vital to brain enhancement. The prevention of Alzheimer's disease and other dementias is another valid reason for memory care.

To look after your mind, you need to develop and maintain your memory skills. Emotion is critical to the formation of memory.

Exercise

What is the key to brain enhancement?

_____

_____

_____

_____

_____

_____

How do you know if your memory is functioning normally or not?

_____

_____

_____

_____

_____

_____

_____

Explain the three bases of memory formation?

_____

_____

_____

_____

_____

_____

_____

_____

_____

Why do you need to care about your memory?

_____

_____

_____

_____

_____

_____

_____

_____

_____

What is "procedural memory"?

_____

_____

_____

_____

_____

_____

_____

_____

_____

Can you trust your memory?

_____

_____

_____

_____

_____

_____

_____

_____

_____

Personal Reflection

Goals & Objectives

_____

_____

_____

_____

_____

_____

_____

_____

_____

Action Plan

_____

_____

_____

_____

_____

_____

_____

_____

_____

TWO
EVOLUTION OF OUR
UNDERSTANDING OF MEMORY

Background

Memory has been written about over the years. The ancients used memory as creative thinking. The Greeks were among the early sects who moved to perfect the faculty of memory. The Egyptians then fostered the evolution of reading. Eventually, Europe embraced memory concepts, including concentration and repetition.

Currently, a lot has changed as regards the knowledge of memory, including underlying principles.

Exercise

What was the key principle of Simonides' memory method?

_____

_____

_____

_____

_____

_____

Who were the first to use special techniques to perfect the faculty of memory?

_____

_____

_____

_____

_____

_____

_____

_____

_____

How does Boncompagno da Signa define memory?

_____

_____

_____

_____

_____

_____

_____

_____

_____

What are the mental states that prevent the creation of a strong memory?

_____

_____

_____

_____

_____

_____

_____

_____

What is the difference between short-term memory and long-term memory?

_____

_____

_____

_____

_____

_____

_____

_____

List the three principles which underlie the formation, retention, and recall of a memory.

_____

_____

_____

_____

_____

_____

_____

_____

Personal Reflection

Goals & Objectives

_____

_____

_____

_____

_____

_____

_____

_____

_____

Action Plan

_____

_____

_____

_____

_____

_____

_____

_____

_____

THREE
DIFFERENT TYPES OF MEMORY

<u>Background</u>

Memory is the basis of identity. With different types, memory can be divided into transient and long-term.

Transient sensory memory refers to the memory we have when remembering for a few seconds what we have just seen, heard, tasted or felt. Except you make a deliberate effort to retain its created impression, it disappears easily.

Long-term memories are the opposite. They include episodic, semantic, procedural memory.

Exercise

What causes us not to remember our childhood before ages two and three?

_____

_____

_____

_____

_____

_____

Define 'chunking'.

_____

_____

_____

_____

_____

_____

_____

_____

_____

_____

What is Sir James Jeans' representation of pi?

_____

_____

_____

_____

_____

_____

_____

Explain the Zeigarnik Effect.

_____

_____

_____

_____

_____

_____

_____

_____

_____

_____

_____

_____

Explain what you understand by "working memory".

_____

_____

_____

_____

_____

_____

_____

Outline the principal activities meditated by the frontal lobes.

_____

_____

_____

_____

_____

_____

_____

_____

_____

_____

Personal Reflection

_____

_____

_____

_____

_____

_____

_____

_____

_____

_____

_____

_____

_____

_____

_____

_____

_____

_____

_____

_____

_____

_____

_____

Goals & Objectives

_____
_____
_____
_____
_____
_____
_____
_____
_____

Action Plan

_____
_____
_____
_____
_____
_____
_____
_____
_____

FOUR
MEMORY IN ACTION

<u>Background</u>

Learning a new language is an example of the brain in action. Learning is linked with episodic, implicit and procedural memories.

Deep processing, forcing the brain to work harder and duplicating are processes that increase the chances for later recall.

Using catchphrases is the easiest and most common way of memorizing. Rhyming acronyms being the most effective.

Exercise

Which of the memory systems is most prone to error?

_____

_____

_____

_____

_____

_____

_____

_____

_____

How do catchphrases aid in memorization?

_____

_____

_____

_____

_____

_____

_____

_____

Why should we use larger screens when studying information?

_____

_____

_____

_____

_____

_____

_____

_____

_____

What is Herbert Simon's input on intuition?

_____

_____

_____

_____

_____

_____

_____

_____

Describe the process of human memory maturity.

_____

_____

_____

_____

_____

_____

_____

_____

_____

What feature evolve in line with the development of the frontal lobes?

_____

_____

_____

_____

_____

_____

_____

_____

_____

_____

Personal Reflection

Goals & Objectives

_____
_____
_____
_____
_____
_____
_____
_____
_____
_____

Action Plan

_____
_____
_____
_____
_____
_____
_____
_____
_____
_____
_____

FIVE
WHAT CAN GO WRONG

Background

There are stumbling blocks that can lead to distorted memories. Absent-mindedness, bias, blocking, misattribution, transience, suggestibility, persistence are some examples.

These could lead to forgetfulness. The way the brain operates, only things that are important or might be important in the future are remembered, unimportant things are forgotten.

Exercise

Mention the first seven stumbling blocks that lead to lost or distorted memories.

_____

_____

_____

_____

_____

_____

_____

_____

Explain the attributes of distorted memories stumbling blocks.

_____

_____

_____

_____

_____

_____

_____

_____

What does Daniel Schachter refer to as 'source amnesia'?

_____

_____

_____

_____

_____

_____

_____

_____

_____

Explain the eighth enemy of memory.

_____

_____

_____

_____

_____

_____

_____

_____

_____

What is forgetfulness?

_____

_____

_____

_____

_____

_____

_____

_____

What three processes did S. use to enhance his memory?

_____

_____

_____

_____

_____

_____

_____

_____

Personal Reflection

_____

_____

_____

_____

_____

_____

_____

_____

_____

_____

_____

_____

_____

_____

_____

_____

_____

_____

_____

_____

_____

_____

_____

_____

_____

_____

_____

Goals & Objectives

_____
_____
_____
_____
_____
_____
_____
_____
_____

Action Plan

_____
_____
_____
_____
_____
_____
_____
_____
_____
_____

SIX
THE PROMISES AND PERILS OF MEMORY

Background

Creativity thrives where there are clearly remembered images. Closely associated to creativity is the memory for dreams. Equally related are memory and imagination. As we progress in our ability to imagine, our memories are strengthened.

This leads to the feeling of familiarity, often associated with shared experiences.

<u>Exercise</u>

What is the role of the amygdala?

_____
_____
_____
_____
_____
_____
_____
_____

Why are dramatic and emotionally arousing imaginations the best structure for remembering things?

_____
_____
_____
_____
_____
_____
_____
_____
_____

What is presentism in psychology?

_____

_____

_____

_____

_____

_____

_____

_____

In your own words, define historical memory.

_____

_____

_____

_____

_____

_____

_____

_____

_____

Define memory wars.

_____

_____

_____

_____

_____

_____

_____

_____

_____

What are memory laws?

_____

_____

_____

_____

_____

_____

_____

_____

Personal Reflection

Goals & Objectives

_____

_____

_____

_____

_____

_____

_____

_____

_____

Action Plan

_____

_____

_____

_____

_____

_____

_____

_____

_____

_____

SEVEN
ACCESSORY AIDS TO A BETTER
MEMORY

Background

A number of activities and diets aid better memory. Drugs like Amphetamines help boost short-term memory, but also have adverse effects. Alcohol is equally a substance that leads to decreased memory and dementia.

There are however some reliable memory facilitators which include sleep, diet and exercises.

Exercise

What is the role of 'clusterin'?

_____

_____

_____

_____

_____

_____

_____

_____

What is the ingredient in dark chocolate that improves memory function?

_____

_____

_____

_____

_____

_____

_____

_____

_____

How does sleep enhance memory?

_____

_____

_____

_____

_____

_____

_____

_____

What else can improve memory function apart from food and sleep?

_____

_____

_____

_____

_____

_____

_____

_____

_____

How do you incorporate berries, fermented foods and leafy greens into healthy diets?

_____

_____

_____

_____

_____

_____

_____

_____

How does exercise lower the risk of dementia?

_____

_____

_____

_____

_____

_____

_____

_____

Personal Reflection

Goals & Objectives

_____
_____
_____
_____
_____
_____
_____
_____
_____

Action Plan

_____
_____
_____
_____
_____
_____
_____
_____
_____
_____

Made in the USA
Las Vegas, NV
24 January 2024

84842814R00026